The Nightingale

by Kristin Hannah

: This is a quick read summary based on the book
"The Nightingale"

by Kristin Hannah

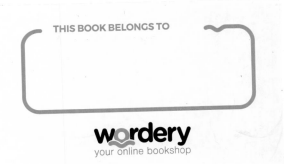

Note to Readers:

This is a Summary & Analysis of "The Nightingale" by Kristin Hannah. You are encouraged to buy the full version.

TABLE OF CONTENT

Introduction

Brief/Vague Summary of entire Novel

Settings for the story

Story Plot Analysis

How to Use this Summary

Chapter analysis

Chapters 1-3

Chapters 4-6

Chapters 7-8

Chapters 9-11

Chapters 12-13

Chapters 14-16

Chapters 17-18

Chapters 19-20

Chapters 21-23

Chapter 24-26

Chapters 27-29

Chapter 30-32

Chapters 33-34

Chapters 35-36

Chapters 37-39

Characters

Main

Secondary

Main Character Analysis

Alternate Ending

Symbols

Themes

Real World Truth

Thought provoking moments

Thoughts for a Prequel or a Sequel

Conclusion/Final Analysis

INTRODUCTION

Brief/Vague Summary of entire Novel

It is 1939 in France and rumors and stories of war have begun to sweep the country. Vianne and Isabelle Rossignol are two sisters who couldn't be more alike, and have already suffered the tragedy of loosing their mother to illness and their father to grief and alcohol, and instead of brining them closer this has driven them apart. Vianne, a timid, housewife and mother, refuses to believe war is coming, and does everything in her power to ignore the inevitable, naively believing the war will not touch her and her family. Isabelle on the other hand is a rambunctious, angry, beautiful young woman who is overly eager to join in the war effort to keep France safe. When war breaks out in France however, the two soon learn that they cannot go on behaving the way they have; Vianne has to learn to be tough and strong, her husband having been drafted into the war and a German billeting at her home, Vianne now must learn to take control and be strong for those she loves. Isabelle on the other hand learns that the world is not as black and white as she had believed and that fighting for what she believes in is not nearly as glamorous or easy to do as she originally thought. However, it is through all the following years of war, sacrifice and suffering, that these two women, these sisters, come to realize their true selves and what they are really capable of, and after enduring the hardships of cold, starvation, angry and vicious Germans, unimaginable loss and constant fear for their lives, the two come to see what really matters in life; family, love, forgiveness and a strong sense of self.

SETTINGS FOR THE STORY

The *Nightingale* starts out in the year 1995 in Organ as an elderly Vianne reminisces about her time in the war. The reader is then transported back, as the old woman looks back upon her and her sisters lives, to the years 1939 through the end of World War II, which take place mostly within France, specifically within the cities of Paris and the idyllic fictional town of Carrievau situated in the Loire Valley. Other places mentioned throughout the story include but are not limited to: Spain, the Pyrenees mountains, Germany and the Ravensbruck concentration camp.

STORY PLOT ANALYSIS

This book is written in a third person narrative, allowing for the story to be told in an objective yet captivating way. The focus of the book being split between the Characters Vianne and Isabelle, the reader is taken on a journey of self discovery and bravery via the adventures of Isabelle and the hardships Vianne faces. Throughout the story it becomes clear that Isabelle, strong, brave and stubborn as she is, is the anchor that ties all the characters together. And while Vianne is the focus for much of the story, it is clear that it is Isabelle who brings all the characters together, and helps to bring the story and the character's lives full circle, both thorough the war as well as at the end of the novel when Isabelle, once again and even from the grave, manages to bring everyone she loved together in one place.

HOW TO USE THIS SUMMARY

This summary should be used both as a guide to the story, a reference to be used to brush up on the story with, and a means to further discussion and analysis of a very thought provoking, enthralling and slightly enigmatic book.

CHAPTER ANALYSIS

CHAPTERS 1-3

An elderly woman is introduced as packing up her belongings to move away from her Oregon home on the coast to spend the remainder of her life within a nursing home, via her son's desires; the year is 1995. The woman seems not to mind this much, as she is less interested in her possessions and placement than she is in making her son feel helpful and happy. She does however make it clear that she will not part with one specific belonging; a special truck, shrouded in the mystery, filled with memorabilia, containing, specifically an identification card naming Juliette Gervasie which, upon the woman's accidental slip, her son sees and mentions, and which in turn starts a rush of memories.

The reader is brought back to a time just before France entered World War II (1939), to the French countryside of Loire Valley, where a young woman by the name of Vianne lives with her Husband Antoine and daughter Sophie. Vianne reminisces on how she came to be at this place, when her father dropped both her and her younger sister (Isabelle), off there, at their once summer home, years before to live with a caretaker after their mother's death. Vianne, who was distraught after her mother's death, seemed unable to watch over her younger sister Isabelle, and instead found solace only in Antoine, her lover and then at 17 years of age, husband, and after suffering multiple miscarriages, the two finally received a daughter who lived; Sophie. Despite these hardships however, it is clear that she and her husband love each other greatly and have created a life together in which they find peace, comfort and beauty, a life in which Vianne is desperate not to see changed by war. Unfortunately however, Antoine soon receives a letter stating that he has been drafted and must depart from his family for the war. Vianne is unsettled and greatly upset by this, however, she refutes all possible negative outcomes believing that France has the upper hand—as she discusses with her neighbor and best friend Rachel de Champlain—and soon after this, Vianne sees Antoine off as he reports for his military duty.

CHAPTERS 4-6

Isabelle Rossignol, now 19, is a student at a preparatory school for young women in training to become high class women of society, however she feels extreme discontent to be forced to learn what she deems as trivial pursuits while there is a war going on. Hence, Isabelle gets herself expelled and returns to live with her father in Paris; it is apparent upon arrival however that Isabelle is less than welcome with her father which brings up familiar and deep feelings of abandonment.

Meanwhile Paris experiences an attacked by the Germans. Planes fly over the city, dropping bombs and shooting down civilians with machine guns, forcing many of its citizens into air raid shelters, including Isabelle and her father.

Once emerged from this specific attack, Isabelle's father finds a way to send his daughter away; he tells Isabelle that she is to ride with his friends who will take her to the area near where her sister, Vianne, is located and that she must go to visit her at her home as she is alone with her child; Vianne's husband still being at war. Isabelle refutes this demand with gusto, however in the end is forced to get into the car with her

Father's kin and drive off into the mass crowds of fleeing people who have begun to push their way through the streets.

It is only a short time after this however that the car runs out of petrol and is unable to go any farther—there being no fuel left to sell. And so it is decided that the family and Isabelle will head towards a nearby hotel in order to find a resting place and regroup. No sooner than Isabelle steps out of the car door however, does she become engulfed in the mob of a crowd that has continued to surround them on their journey, and she becomes separated from her hosts and is forced to resort to walking with the crowd itself towards a safer destination.

After what has seemed to be an endless amount of time in her eyes, a tired and starving Isabelle finds herself in a position in which her money can do nothing for her—all rations having been bought up by people much farther ahead of herself on the road—and she must find something to eat. So, overwhelmed by her hunger, she staggers off into the woods, following the smell of cooking on a campfire, until she finds herself in the camp of a former prisoner named Gaetan. While sharing his meal with her, the two discus their situations and eventually come to agree on a mutual plan; they will go and visit both Isabelle's sister as well as Gaetan's mother and will then join the French soldiers to help fight the war.

The next morning Isabelle wakes with her new found friend, and the two set off to attempt to follow through on their plan. After multiple days of walking and exhaustion have set in, Isabelle hears the familiar humming of fighter planes and another attack on France occurs as German planes fly over the crowds of people all attempting to flee and drop bombs and bullets down onto a defenseless crowd. Isabelle and Gaetan attempt to escape this massacre, taking refuge in a near by stone church, hoping to live as the walls and ceiling are torn apart by the plane's and their weapons.

CHAPTERS 7-8

Vianne sits in her classroom with her students who all ask questions about the war and voice the fears they have heard their parents discussing. Vianne attempts to answer as best she can, however it is apparent the she herself is having a hard time not being overcome with fear and anxiety. Even with this however , Vianne seems determined to focus only on positive thoughts and turns to cleaning and work to avoid such negative thoughts. After school Vianne and Rachel walk to their homes with their children and discuss the issues; Rachel states that horrible stories have been circulating regarding the horrors that French people have begun to experience.

Later, after Vianne has put her daughter to bed, she moves to her garden to pull weeds in a further attempt to distract her mind from the worry she feels. She is soon approached by a trio of people who ask her for food and water; she willingly obliges and then is told by the three that she must go inside and lock the doors, for a fleeing mob of people are now arriving in the small town and it is unsafe for her out in the open. Vianne goes into her home, locks all doors and shutters, and soon thereafter fists begin to hammer on her doors and windows, thousands of desperate people begging her for help; she remains silent, not letting anyone in and comforting her daughter who has woken, terrified by the noise.

Meanwhile, Isabelle reaches her sister's home with Gaetan, exhausted and covered in blood, but the two are not let in, and so they move to the back garden to sleep in the pergola. Before sleep Isabelle makes Gaetan promise to take her to fight with him in the war and Gaetan then kisses Isabelle, who in turn pronounces that she loves him.

The next mooring Isabelle is awoken, alone, by Vianne, who baths her and puts her to rest. Once Isabelle has rested enough, she confronts Vianne about France's situation, stating that swastika flags now fly over the Eiffel tower, and Vianne shows Isabelle the note that had been left to her by Gaetan stating "You are not ready"; Isabelle is deeply hurt. This hurt however does not remain the dominate emotion in Isabelle for long; Isabelle has become furious with the Nazi's as well as with France for surrendering, and is desperate to fight back and rebel against the German's new authoritative presence within the town, despite her sister's pleas for her to remain docile and conform so that they may remain unharmed.

Isabelle soon finds however there is not much she can do to help, and so she turns to finding all of her sister's valuables, as well as some provisions, and hiding them in a small hidden room underneath their barn as a small attempt to fight back. Later that night she listens to the radio and hears

General de Gaulle put out a call to action among the French people, asking them not to give up the fight and not to surrender; Isabelle feels a rush to comply.

Soon after, all town residents are called to a meeting in which they are told that they must turn over their radios and any firearms and ammunition, as well as abide by a strict 9pm curfew, and if they choose not to do this, the penalty will by immediate death by execution.

Further enraged, Isabelle returns home with her sister and niece, only to find that a German soldier by the name of Captain Wolfgang Beck will be moving into their home. In protest Isabelle chops off her waist length hair, and Vianne begs her to control herself around Beck, lest he decided to shoot them all.

Vianne, Sophie, Isabelle and Captain Beck all proceed to have dinner together, although it is a very uncomfortable one, with Isabelle being as rude as possible to Captain Beck and Vianne being anxious and fearful. After the dinner finally ends Vianne goes out into the garden to try to calm herself and is met by Captain Beck who keeps making remarks that seem to make him appear more human and kind than Vianne would like to think of him as, as he is the enemy. Isabelle on the other hand decides that she cannot reside in a house which is also occupied by the enemy of her country and leaves for the train station. Her efforts however are soon proven fruitless as travel between countries has been banned unless one is granted a pass. So she returns home to her sister's house who then makes it clear that she is not to cause trouble and is to go to town to buy their rations each day.

A week has passed, and Isabelle feels as if she is a bomb waiting to go off at the Germans. While in town she finds a piece of chalk as she waits in line for rations. She then uses this chalk to deface German propaganda posters, however is caught but what she believes, at first, to be the German police. It turns out however that she has instead been discovered by a small resistance group who poses as the German police to find possible other members, and she soon agrees to help the group out by secretly delivering resistance propaganda to the towns people, somethings she is very excited about doing, however is punishable by death if discovered. Despite this very real possible consequence however, Isabelle wakes at 4am the next morning and distributes all her material to varying households through the town.

She continues to do this every morning, and while she is able to remain uncaught, Vianne begins to notice Isabelle's frequent absence. She wrongly assumes however that Isabelle is sneaking out early to meet a boy.

Meanwhile, Captain Beck confronts Vianne, telling her that he has acquired information about her, and many of the other townswoman's husbands; they have all been captured and taken as prisoners of war and will not be returning home. Vianne then takes it upon herself to inform the other women, finding postcards for them all to write to their husbands on. She then returns to her home to find Captain Beck at her table; in return for finding information on her husband's whereabouts and sending the letters, Captain Beck asks Vianne to write down on a piece of paper, the names of any and all of the freemasons, jews, homosexuals or communists that work in her school. While he presents the request as a choice, Vianne knows that this is just a courtesy and that if she were to refuse she not only would be kicked out of her own home, but possibly worse. So she obliges and writes down all the names. When she finishes Captain Beck reminds her that she has forgotten one name, and Vianne is forced to write down "Rachel de Champlain".

CHAPTERS 12-13

It is now mid November; the weather has become dangerously cold and the money and rations are running out. As Vianne sits in the early morning hours knitting a scarf for her daughters Christmas present, Isabelle attempts to sneak back into the house after having finished her early morning deliveries of resistance propaganda. She is caught by Vianne who has grown steadily more suspicious of her sister, believing her to be leading a secret love life. Isabelle denies this half-heartedly and proceeds to leave again, this time for town to collect their rations.

Soon after, Rachel appears at Vianne's door, and reminds her that there is still school that day and Vianne, running late, rushes to get to her job on time.

While Vianne and the other teachers are at school with the children, a car with German police show up in the cold yard. They inform Vianne that they are there to let some of the school's teachers go, specifically the jews, freemasons, and communists, including, to Vianne's great dismay, Rachel.

Vianne feels horribly guilty after this, as it was her who provided the list of name from which the Nazis had used to fire many of her colleagues, and after attempting to fix the solution by paying a visit to Captain Beck which proved unsuccessful,

Vianne finally comes to the conclusion that she must, at the very least, come clean to her friend Rachel and ask for forgiveness and never make such a rash "stupid" decision again.

Fast forward to April of 1941. Isabelle receives a cryptic note stating she must immediately go and meet with the resistance group she has joined. Her sister however mistakenly takes this as a note for Isabelle to go and meet her secret lover, who she believes to be Henri, as he was the one to deliver the message, and greatly disapproves due to the dangers of associating with a known communist. Isabelle however is unaffected by this, and immediately leaves to meet with her group.

Once she has arrived, Henri and the others in the group tell Isabelle that they need someone to go to Paris to deliver a message to their Parisian resistance group leader, as well as someone who can stay there and act as a sort of currier between the two groups for some time. Isabelle agrees to the task, needing only to find a way to obtain a pass to travel before she can go.

When she arrives home, she arrives to a house who's stone fence has been demolished and who's contents are being looted by German soldiers. She doesn't remark too much on any of this however and proceeds to ask Captain Beck if he would be able to help her procure a travel pass to go and nurse her "sick" father. He agrees, though a now worried Vianne corners her sister afterward, confused as to why she herself did not know her father was ill. Isabelle however is ready for this and tells Vianne that their father is fine and that she is actually going to Paris to spend some time alone with Henri; and while her sister is horribly angered by this, stating that Isabelle is foolish and selfish, she believes her.

CHAPTERS 14-16

Fast forwarding again to 1995, the old woman moves into the residential section of a senior living home with the help of her son. Upon settling in, her son hands her some of her mail. She goes through it and seems shocked to find what appears to be an invitation for a reunion for people who helped in World War II, an invitation for "Passeurs".

Back in Carriveau in 1941, Conditions in the town are continually worsening and all of the Jewish members have been forced out of work. Vianne on the other hand finds her life is a bit easier with her sister gone; she no longer has to worry about Isabelle loosing her temper in front of Captain Beck, or saying something that would get them all into trouble. Despite this however, Vianne shows signs of missing Isabelle. Captain Beck on the other hand obviously feels much more at ease and free to communicate with Vianne without Isabelle in the home, becoming very friendly with both Vianne and her daughter and even delivering her a letter from Antoine. Despite this however, Vianne tries to constantly reminds herself that she must not trust Captain Beck, that he is the enemy and that he is extremely dangerous; even knowing this fact she seems to struggle with keeping his civility at bay.

Meanwhile in Paris Isabelle successfully delivers her first currier letter for the resistance group and convinces her father to let her stay with him in Paris despite his obvious disgust with the idea. She also reopens her Father's old book shop as a pretense for her fellow Resistance colleagues to contact her at, after having attended a meeting where she met the leader of the Paris portion of the resistance group, and her Father's former friend, M'sieur Levy, among others. Here she is warned against the "collabos" (French citizens who work for the Nazis).

While at this same meeting, a hurt member of the British Royal Air Force is brought into the meeting place. The group agrees to help the man recover and to try to find a way to get him out of France and back to Britain, despite the fact that this means risking all of their lives.

CHAPTERS 17-18

Back in Carrievau Vianne has run out of money and has been fired from her teaching position for asking too many questions, leaving her without even her small salary to fall back on. Vianne become extremely worried about how she and her daughter will be able to survive in the coming winter with no money. When she arrives home Captain Beck confronts her, sensing she is upset and she reveals what has happened. He in return promises her, in a bordering on romantic way, that he would never let Sophie go hungry.

In Paris Isabelle has taken easily to running the bookshop. She flirts with the German soldiers, keeping them in the dark while Anouk delivers resistance messages to her right under the German's noses. One night on her way home, Isabelle discovers a British Air Force member hiding in a large urn. His plane had gone down some days before and he had been hiding out there ever since. She makes a quick decision to help this man out, and tells him to meet her at her apartment, (which she gives him the address for) in one hour. When the man, named Lieutenant Torrance MacLeish, arrives at her home, she quickly hides him in the hidden room behind her armoire and then leaves to dispose of his uniform and tags in the Seine river.

The next morning Isabelle takes the man to meet her Resistance colleagues, and though they are surprised by the man, they agree that some sort of plan must be devised to get both Lieutenant MacLeish and the other British Air Force pilot out of France and back to Britain. Anouk suggest that they smuggle the two men into Spain via the Pyrenees Mountains, though this would be a very dangerous task and the one to do it would most likely be unable to lead a normal life or trust anyone thereafter. Isabelle however, fully aware of the risks and hardships this journey would likely bring, offers to be the one to shepherd the two men into Spain, and after a few moments quiet deliberation the group agree. By this time Gaetan has appeared, taking Isabelle completely off guard as all her feeling for the man come rushing back. This however does not stop the group; M'sieur Levy informs Gaetan that they will need money immediately if they are to follow through with the plan, and upon this Gaetan takes his leave, presumably to set up a way to fund the trip.

Over the next six hours the group plan a route, set up safe houses and develop a full blown plan to be executed by Isabelle and the two soldiers. Before she knows it however, the cities curfew is upon them and Isabelle takes her leave. When she finally arrives at her apartment Gaetan is there waiting for her. Isabelle asks him why he left her, to which he responded with "because I wanted to forget you", and touching her face, he says goodbye.

Once inside the apartment Isabelle is immediately confronted by her Father, who chastises her for being late. After this however he confesses that he knows she has helped a British Air Force Lieutenant. Confused Isabelle denies everything, but her Father continues on to tell her that he also knows that she came to Paris to join the resistance, that she has been working with them for some time, that he knows about the journey she intends to embark on, and that he too is in fact a member; he was the one who had been creating the resistance propaganda Isabelle had been passing out for the last several months.

Chapters 19-20

It is months later and Isabelle's group of downed pilots—which has now grown to include four men and herself—are ready to leave. The five of them take a train to Luz and then proceed to the base of the Pyrenees mountains where they meet with and convince a man by the name of Eduardo to guide them over the mountains and into Spain. The journey is very dangerous, and the five and their guide are faced with freezing temperatures, exhaustion and hunger, but finally they make it into Spain safely, going straight to the British Consulate. From there they speak with the Counsel who is deeply impressed by the rescue and offers to fund future rescues while simultaneously making the operation a legitimate one.

Isabelle, who at one point sense that Gaetan is around and watching her, continues to make these trips back and fourth through the Pyrenees, and begins to become famous for her work, always operating under the name Juliette and Nightingale.

Vianne on the other hand is continuing to struggle to get by in the hard winter, selling off the remainder of her belongings and giving all the food she can find to her daughter Sophie, taking none for herself. Thus she falls ill, and on the way home from church one Sunday afternoon become too weak to continue walking, falls, and hits her head hard on the pavement. Sophie, terrified for her mother, runs to find Captain Beck who carries Vianne home and watches over her until Rachel is able to make it to the house. A day later Vianne wakes and Captain Beck forces her to eat the food he has brought with him, lest she die and Sophie be left with nobody to care for her.

Months later in Spring, Vianne is Gardening when Sarah (Rachel's daughter) runs to Vianne's home begging her to come help her mother who seems to have completely given up. When Vianne arrives at Rachel's home it is to find Rachel sitting on her back porch completely dejected; the new Government has now decided that all Jews must purchase and wear a yellow star of David on all of their outerwear henceforth to identify themselves as Jews. Everyone is scared.

CHAPTERS 21-23

Sophie has taken ill, she has a fever that will most likely kill her if she doesn't get help; Vianne, as ever, worries. Captain Beck however appears and offers Vianne antibiotic for her daughter which she accepts, fully knowing that in doing so she now may owe the Captain a favor.

Concurrently, Isabelle continues to move downed AFE soldiers out of France and back home to their countries, although she is warned that the Germans are now very aware that this is happening and are keen to find "the Nightingale" responsible.

Later Anouk sends Isabelle to a German building where women have gathered to work. Upon her arrival she finds that Germans are gathering the names and addresses of all foreign born Jewish citizens. She then promptly leaves to return home to discuss this finding with her Father. It is in the middle of this discussion however that warning is slipped underneath their door, alerting them to the fact that all foreign born Jews are to be rounded up and deported. With only a brief talk it is decided between the two that they will try to hid who they can before this occurs to keep them safe. They then proceed to Ruth Freedman's home—a Jewish woman who resides in the building—and ask her and her children to come and hide in their hidden room to stay safe; they do. Isabelle then proceeds to Lily Vizniak's home (another Jewish woman in the building), but is too late; the police got their first and proceed to take Lily and her children away. Isabelle, upset, follows the police to try to get answers, and discovers that all the Jews that the police round up are being deported to work camps in Germany and are to be shot immediately if they attempt to escape.

Life for Jews in Carrievau is not much better; so many new restrictions have been set in place making it almost impossible for Jews to exist within the town. After a day in the town Isabelle arrives at Rachel's home and shares the little food she was able to attain in the town that day, as Rachel is no longer allowed in the town to shop expect for one hour in the late afternoon when all the food is already gone. While the two women sit and visit, Captain Beck comes to Rachel's door and warns them, at risk to his career, that Rachel must not be home tomorrow morning or she will be taken away.

Heeding the Captains advice, Rachel takes her children and together with Vianne, leaves her home and sets out for the free zone portion of France. When the group gets to the checkpoint Rachel and her children say goodbye to Vianne and must then attempt to cross with their fake papers through the border. Sadly however they are discovered and while running away Sarah—Rachel's daughter—is shot and killed. The women however have no time to mourn this and rush, with Sarah's body as well as Ari—Rachel's son—back home to Vianne's house. Once arrived, Vianne forces Rachel and Ari to hide in her farm cellar while she buries Sarah next to her own mother in the garden.

The next morning Vianne keeps Rachel hidden and goes into town with Sophie. She expects to see turmoil and trouble but all seems normal. Upon returning home Vianne tells Sophie of the horrible news; the her best friend, Sarah, had died the night before. Sophie, devastated, becomes furious; she is no longer an innocent child and is beginning to truly understand the devastating effects of the war; she then leaves her mother alone in the garden, returning to the house. Vianne then proceeds to let Rachel out of the cellar. She believes it is safe enough for her to come for a few moments to allow Rachel and her son to cleanup. This however was a grievous mistake, as seconds after Rachel emerges she is picked up by a collaborator and is forced into the car that is to take her to the train station. Vianne however, distraught, insists on coming with her. Once they arrive at the train station Vianne sees thousands of Jews being forced onto trains and Captain Beck standing in the middle with a whip. Before she can process this too much however, Rachel is ushered onto a train. Not before she is able to hand Ari off to Vianne however and beg her to take care of her son which Vianne promises to do. The two then wave goodbye and Rachel is lost to view.

Vianne returns home, where Captain Beck soon meets her. Vianne is upset but realizes that Captain Beck did attempt to warn her of what would happen to prevent her friend from being taken. He then promises that he will protect Vianne, Sophie and Ari, and the two share a desire to kiss each other.

CHAPTER 24-26

Isabelle meets with Anouk who informs her that she is to deliver a message to Henri in Carrievau. She also lets it slip that Gaetan will be there and that he often speaks of her. Vianne on the other hand has taken over the care of Ari, but worries because it is rumored that soon even French born Jews will begin to be deported. Captain Beck knows this and helps Vianne out by getting her fake papers for Ari. Vianne then begins to tell people that she has adopted one of her husband's family members children as the mother died in Childbirth. Ari's new name becomes Daniel and Vianne hopes this will be enough to keep him safe.

When Isabelle arrives in Carrievau, she goes to Henri's hotel and is informed that there is to be a secrete meeting that night, she is also informed, again, that the search for "the Nightingale" has increased and that the Germans are frantic to find her. Later that night Isabelle sneaks out of the Hotel (as it is after the city curfew) to attend the meeting. On her way there however the local German airfield is bombed by American fighter planes one of which goes down. Vianne then goes in search of the pilot, finds him badly injured and attempts to get him—with the help of Gaetan and Henri who have show up to the scene to help—to a safe location. She chooses her sister's barn yard cellar as it is the closest. Once there she and the fallen pilot hide and Gaetan and Henri leave to find help.

Later, Captain Beck returns home in a horrible mood. He informs Vianne that a fighter plane has gone down nearby and that the Germans have been unable to find the fallen pilot. He is distraught as he is being blamed for the pilot's apparent disappearance and fears he will be killed for it. When he leaves to search again Vianne notices that the barn door is slightly ajar. Thinking Rachel has returned and hidden she rushes to the cellar and opens the door. She is shocked however to find, not Rachel, but Isabelle and the pilot captain Beck has just mentioned. Furious and terrified she instructs Isabelle to be gone by the morning and never return. Subsequently Captain Beck returns home, at a complete loss, and then, out of desperation begins to search Vianne's own home. When Captain Beck makes his way to the barn yard cellar Vianne panics, and just as he opens the door she hits Captain Beck in the head with a shovel while Isabelle simultaneously shoots him in the chest. Beck dies, but not before firing his own gun at Isabelle who collapses. Henri and Gaetan have arrived by this time and after briefly explaining what has happened, it is agreed that Isabelle will be taken to get help in the free zone and that the two bodies (Captain Beck's and the pilot's), will be disposed of.

Fast forward; it is 1995 in Organ again and the old woman sits contemplating the invitation she has received; it is specifically to honor the work that Juliette Gervaise ("the Nightingale") did throughout the war. After receiving a brief phone call from an event organizer asking if she'll be able to attend, the woman makes a quick decision to leave, books a ticket, packs her bags, phones her son and leaves for home.

Chapters 27-29

Vianne rides with Gaetan to help smuggle Isabelle into the free zone of France in order to recover; they both profess that they love Isabelle but that it sometimes hard or dangerous to show. Once Vianne sees that Gaetan has safely made it across the check point she return home to await the Germans that will inevitably come to question her about Beck's whereabouts. Both men have been buried.

When the German soldiers eventually come to Vianne's house, they take her away for questioning. She tells them that Captain Beck came home two days before, extremely agitated, having been unable to find the fallen pilot, and then suddenly declared he knew where the pilot was and immediately took off and that she hadn't seen him since. The Germans seem to believe this. However now there is an empty room in Vianne's home, and a new German, Sturmbannfuhrer Von Richter, declares that he will billet there instead. Upon Strumbannfuhrer's arrival, he takes the best room and blanket in the home, proving himself to be a cruel and vindictive, power hungry, individual. Vianne is terrified that he will discover the truth about Ari.

Isabelle meanwhile, safe in the free zone, finally wakes up. Gaetan has stayed entire time and he informs her that her sister is safe for now but that she is refusing to go into hiding. The two, in their way, profess their feelings for each other, and later become intimate.

Vianne meanwhile is conflicted and scared, frequently having nightmares about all her worries as the tension in her home grows ever thinker. About a week later Vianne finally decides to take Ari into town with her to introduce him as Daniel. After standing in queues all day with little success Vianne decides it is time to go home, however all the streets seem to be barricaded; the Germans are rounding up Jews and deporting them, foreign born or not. A jewish woman by the name of Helen Ruelle reaches out to Vianne last minute begging her to take her four year old son Jean Georges and save him from deportation. Vianne does and she returns home with Sophie, Daniel and Jean Georges. Upon her return home Strumbannfuhrer informs her that he will be leaving as the free zone in France will now become occupied with Germans as well. He also instructs her to take the child to the orphanage.

Upon arrive at the orphanage the sisters take in the young boy even though it is a great risk, and it is then decided that Vianne and the sisters will set up an operation attempting to save as many refugee children as possible; Vianne is to be the leader.

Isabelle on the other hand has almost completely recovered and the precious time she has spent with Gaetan will soon be at an end.

CHAPTER 30-32

Entering the city together Isabelle and Gaetan come to find that France no longer has a free zone. Gaetan then informs Isabelle that he will be leaving their resistance group to join a guerrilla warfare group; he wants to being to physically fight. Isabelle will continue to escort fallen airmen through the Pyrenees despite the increasing risk.

Vianne meanwhile works with Henri to set up her child saving operation. Henri gives Vianne fake papers for Jean George and Vianne learns to forge documents while also devising a way of keeping track of who each child she saves is so that they may be retuned to their parents after the war. She also accepts a position in the Orphanage as a teacher to explain her continued presence there.

It is now 1995 again, and the old woman sits in the airport, her plane delayed. Soon her son arrives, not willing to let his mother travel in her state on her own. Everyone boards the plane and the woman promises her son that she will tell him what she has been hiding all these years, but first, she wishes to take a nap. They leave for France.

Now it is May of 1944. It has been 18 months since German invaded the rest of France and took over the free zones. Isabelle meets with her Father and receives several fake identity papers from him and tells him that Vianne and Sophie are safe. Isabelle then travels to see Gaetan. It has been eight months since they last saw each other and this meeting is to be, as all the previous, a sort of good-bye; Isabelle will be crossing the Pyrenees again at ever increased risk, and Gaetan is to go on an extremely dangerous mission with his guerrilla group (known as the Maquis).

The next morning Gaetan has left and Isabelle leaves for Madame Babineau's home to begin her next rescue mission. However, once at the house, as the two women and three airmen prepare to leave, German soldiers burst through Madame Babineau's door and the entire group are arrested.

Back in Carrievau Vianna has continued her work to save Jewish children; she has rescued 13. While teaching at the orphanage one day, Sturmbannfuhrer Von Richter interrupts her classroom and brings her in for questioning. He informs her that Henri has been arrested for working with a resistance group and that she, Vianne, has been seen with him. Vianne denies any connection with Henri, and Sturmbannfuhrer Von Richter tells Vianne that if he discovers that she is lying to him he will punish her and enjoy it.

CHAPTERS 33-34

Isabelle is held as a prisoner and tortured. The Germans believes that she knows who the Nightingale is and they want her to name *him*. She realizes they do not know who she is and keeps quite, insisting that she is Juliette Gervasie. She holds out and doesn't give away any information but is severely tortured because of it.

Meanwhile in Carrievau, Vianne's father shows up and tells Vianne that he is sorry for the way he treated her and her sister as children and that he loves her. He then confess that he is going to go to the Germans and turn himself in in an attempt to save Isabelle. Vianne is devastated by the news. She doesn't have long to think about this however for as soon as she returns home she is confronted by Sturmbannfuhrer Von Richter, who has discovered that Daniel is not her real son (although he still doesn't know the boy is Jewish). He threatens to send Daniel away and then begins to man-handle Vianne. It is clear that she will have to let him do what he wants if she hopes to keep her children safe and at home with her. Sturmbannfuhrer Von Richter then proceeds to brutally rape Vianne.

The next day and back in Paris, Julien turns himself in, claiming to be the Nightingale. Isabelle sees this and begs her father to stop, screaming that she is in fact the Nightingale, but nobody believes her. Her father is taken to the town square and set before a firing squad. Just before they kill him he mouths to Isabelle that he loves her.

While this is going on Vianne is on her way to Paris to try to help her father and sister. When she arrives however she is too late. She sees her dead father, as well as Isabelle, who is being taken to the train station to be shipped off to a concentration camp. Isabelle is then shoved into a cramped boxcar with many other women and children. There she finds Madame Babineau who reveals that her real name is Micheline and that she has known who Isabelle is from the beginning. The two embrace as the train makes its way to Ravensbruck camp. Once there the women are stripped down, washed, shaved, and herded into the bunks. They are humiliated and exhausted but try to remain undefeated.

CHAPTERS 35-36

Months have passed and the Allied troops have begun to win the war, and while this is good news in general, it makes Sturmbannfuhrer Von Richter angrier than ever, and he takes out this anger on Vianne, continually beating and raping her. Vianne takes all of it in an attempt to keep her children safe, Sophie however is no longer a young child and is able to guess easily what is going on. One day, while Vianne is teaching at the orphanage, she realizes that she has become pregnant. Their is only one man who's child it could be; Sturmbannfuhrer Von Richter.

Soon after this realization however Sturmbannfuhrer Von Richter announces that he will be leaving their home; all of the Germans are leaving Carrievau.

Only one month after the Germans have left Carrievau, Antoine returns home. He tells Vianne that he escaped the prison he was held in. She, although happy to have him back, worries about what he would think of her if she told him that she had been raped. She feels so much shame and realizes that the two have suffered enough; she chooses not to tell Antoine what has happened to her.

Two months later, she reveals to Antoine that she is pregnant; she lets him believe that it is his. He chooses to see the child as a blessing and implores Vianne to do the same. They profess that they still love each other, despite all that is now between them, and Vianne vows silently that she will find a way back to him.

Meanwhile, Isabelle has been held at her concentration camp for over eight months. She and Micheline continue to support each other, every day just trying to make it to the next. They are treated horribly and live in conditions that will kill them sooner or later. They have however heard rumors of Allied successes and know the war is drawing to a close. It is a matter of time before Germany falls; Isabelle only wishes to remain alive long enough to see a free France.

Eventually Isabelle and Micheline are moved to a new camp for unknown reasons. The journey nearly kills Isabelle but she persists. At the new camp she gets to see a glimpse of Anouk, who informs her that Henri, Paul, Gaetan and the whole group have been arrested and Henri hanged; she has no information on the others. Isabelle is then forced away as Anouk tells her good-bye. Isabelle attempts to reciprocate, but has nothing left.

CHAPTERS 37-39

France begins to recover, the people and cities finally starting to show signs of life again, and Vianne, Antoine and Sophie make their way to Paris in an attempt to find their lost loved ones. There they find out that Rachel and her husband Marc both died and that nobody seems to know who or where Isabelle is. Deeply saddened by all of this, Vianne gives her list of saved children over to a Red Cross worker who promises he'll do what he can to reunite the families.

The three go home and attempt to pick up the pieces of their lives.

One summer afternoon Sophie, Daniel and Antoine put on a show for Vianne, who finally is beginning to feel a semblance of normalcy. Promptly after her family has finished with their performance however two men show up at their home. They tell Vianne and Antoine that they have found Daniel's—Ari's—family in America, and that Ari must be returned to them. Heartbroken, Vianne reluctantly agrees, knowing that it is the right thing to do in the long run, and sends Ari away with the men to meet his family.

Finally Isabelle is rescued, her camp having been liberated, though she is extremely week and ill. She is taken to a hospital and then sent home to Carrievau, where Vianne picks her up at the train station, takes her home and attempts to nurse her back to health. She reads the letter that their father left to the two of them, which states that he is so sorry for not being a father to the two of them and that he did truly love them with all of his "damaged heart"; these are the words that Isabelle has longed her entire life to hear. Later that week, Isabelle sits in the garden with Sophie, her health continuing to decline, when Gaetan appears; he promised that he wold find her when the war was over and now he has. The two embrace and express their undying love for each other.

It is 1995, and the old woman and her son walk the streets of Paris on their way to the reunion. The woman is reminded of her childhood and feels nostalgic, at home and happy. When they finally reach the reunion it is revealed that the old woman is Vianne, and that they are all their to honor her sister Isabelle. After Vianne gives a speech, it is revealed that Isabelle died in the arms of Gaetan moments after he had returned for her, but that she died happy. It is also revealed that about fifteen years prior to this reunion Sophie had died of cancer. Later that evening Vianne runs into Gaetan himself, who introduces her to his daughter, named Isabelle, and confess that he never stopped loving Vianne's sister. Vianne also runs into Ari, who tells her that he is grateful for all that she did for him, loves her and never forgot her or Sophie. Ari also tells Julien that Vianne was a hero herself, having saved him and 19 other Jewish children throughout the war. Julien is impressed and shocked at how little he actually knows about his own mother, and Vianne promises to tell Julien about her entire life. She will however, keep one secret, the secret of Julien's biological father. She thinks to herself that this doesn't really matter anyway, as Antoine had been Julien's father in every way that mattered. She tells Julien that he saver her, her marriage to his father, and their family, and brought everyone back to life.

CHARACTERS

MAIN

-Vianne Mauriac: elderly woman and sister to Isabelle.

-Isabelle Rossignol (aka Juliette Gervasie, aka "the Nightingale"): Vianne's younger sister and the stories protagonist

SECONDARY

-Sophie: Vianne and Antoine's Daughter

-Gaetan Dubois: Isabelle's lover and fellow member of the resistance

-Julien Rossignol: Vianne and Isabelle's father

-Antoine: Vianne's Husband

-Rachel de Champlain: Vianne's best friend and neighbor

-Sarah: Vianne's student and Sophie's friend and Rachel's daughter

-Ari (aka Daniel): Rachel's son/Vianne's adopted son

-Monsieur Quillian: Another next door neighbor of Vianne's

-Madame Dufour: Isabelle's prep school teacher

-Madame Allard: Isabelle's school's headmistress

-Christophe: Isabelle's Paris University friend

-Monsieur Humbert: Julien Rossignol's friend

-Patricia: Monsieur Humbert's wife

-Gilles Fourneir: Vianne's student

-Francois: Another student of Vianne's

-Strumbannfuhrer: One of Hitler's soldiers

-Captain Wolfgang Beck: Soldier staying n Vianne's home

-Marechal Petain: France's leader

-Henri Navarre: Isabelle's fellow resistance member

-Didier: Isabelle's fellow resistance member

-Madam Fournier: a townswoman

-Helene Ruelle: Townswoman/bakers wife

-Julien: Vianne's son

-Anouk: Isabelle's first Paris contact and fellow member of resistance group in Paris

-M'sieur Levy: Leader of revolt group in paris

-Lieutenant Torrance Macleish: Royal Air Force pilot Isabelle saves

-Madame Babineau (aka Micheline): Isabelle's guide safe house holder in Bayonne France, fellow resistance member and friend

-Eduardo: Isabelle's guide through he Pyrenees and resistance member

-Ian (aka "Tuesday"): Contact in Spain at the British Console

-Father Joseph: Priest at local church in Carrievau

-Mother Superior Marie-Therese: Nun that helps Vianne hide and save Jewish children

-Captain Ed Perkins: Downed AFE pilot Isabelle helps

-Ian Trufford: Downed AFE pilot Isabelle helps and later main contact

-Ruth Friedman: Jewish woman in Julian's apartment building that Julian hinds in secret room

-Lily Vizniak: Jewish woman in Julian's apartment building

-Lieutenant Keith Johnson: Fallen pilot Isabelle attempts to save in Carrievau

-Sturmbannfuhrer Von Richter: German to interrogate Vianne after Beck's death and second German to billet at Vianne's home

-Helen Ruelle: Jewish woman in Carrievau that is deported and leaves her son to Vianne

-Jean Georges: Boy Vianne takes to the orphanage and starts her work at saving children

-Major Tom Dowd: Fallen airman Isabelle helps

-Major Jack Foley: Fallen airman Isabelle helps

-Sergeant Smythe: Fallen airman Isabelle helps

-Rittmeister Schmidt: German to interrogate Isabelle

MAIN CHARACTER

ANALYSIS

Isabelle:

Isabelle is just a girl on the cusp of womanhood when the story begins. At just nineteen she has already experienced pain and loss in the forms of her mother's death, her fathers refusal to be a father and her older sister walking away from being a part of Isabelle's life, and suffers from deep abandonment issues. The feelings evoked by said issues however are clearly a major factor in what spurs her to want to take immediate and brave, all though also reckless, action in regards to her desire to help save France, because while she has felt her entire life that she has to look out for herself, that she has nobody to count on but herself, she has always had one one constant: France. Also, because she has had to look out for herself for her entire life, and has done so in a reckless way—rarely caring about the consequences and always seeming to find a way to squeeze herself out of trouble—being more concerned with instant gratification, it would then easily fallow that she would act upon her desire to take immediate action to protect her country in much the same way as she has always acted to protecting herself.

Throughout the story however Isabelle learns, sometimes the hard way, that this sort of action does not always work out for the best, and that sometimes there is good reason to be cautious and even a little bit afraid. And so you see a girl spurred by her insecurities and passions transform into a woman who is motivated by love for others and a deep devotion to a cause she truly believes is bigger than herself, and through her efforts and eventual selfless action, she not only is able to become a major hero for her country, but also able to make peace with both her Father and Sister and comes to find an inner peace within herself. At the end of the story, she is truly happy, at peace, in love, loved and supported by all those around her.

Vianne:

Vianne is possibly the exact opposite of Isabelle at the start of the novel. A bit older, Vianne has a young daughter and husband and is completely dependent on others, both in regards to every day life as well as for her own happiness. For, while Isabelle took the loss of her mother and abandonment of her father and turned it into a sort of independence, Vianne took these same events and became completely dependent on the love of her first and only love Antoine and best friend Rachel, and without them she feels like she has no strength and wouldn't survive. Survive she must however, as eventually both her Husband and best friend are taken away from her via the war and she is left, alone, to care, not only for her own daughter, but also for Rachel's son with whom she has been entrusted.

Throughout the novel we see Vianne struggle with all of this. We see that she is desperate and will do almost anything to avoid believing that she is going to have to experience tremendous suffering and loss and somehow find the strength to continue on. For months she convinces herself that her husband will be home soon and that once there he will tell her how to get through and survive. When this doesn't happen however, and years begin to pass, Vianne is forced to transform into something she never knew she could be: a strong, loving, independent, capable and even brave, woman who can and will survive.

ALTERNATE ENDING

Isabelle lives:

Imagine if, instead of dying just as things came together, Isabelle had lived? What would that have looked like for both Isabelle and Vianne, as well as their family? It is quite possible that had Isabelle lived, she would have become haunted, just as her father had, by both the things she had done as well as seen done throughout the war. Indeed, she already seemed to be exhibiting some small signs of heading in this direction. It is also possible that had she lived Vianne may not have become the person she did in the end. While Vianne absolutely made a difference within the war, one has to wonder what it would have been like to live directly under her sister's legacy. Also, if Isabelle had lived it is very possible that Vianne and her family may never have moved to America, and Vianne may never have got the distance she needed to be able to come to terms with all that had happened.

Despite all these if's and maybe's however, it is tempting to imagine a world in which Isabelle lived and became healthy, healed both her emotional and physical ailments, and gets to marry Gaetan and start a life with him, perhaps having children of their own. Maybe the couple would have moved into a house near by Vianne and her family and the two could have continued to work on their relationship and become a prosperous and happy family tougher.

SYMBOLS

<u>Nightingale:</u> perhaps the most obvious as well as relevant symbol. The nightingale throughout time has been a symbol of beauty, of immortality, of yearning and freedom from the world's troubles, as well as being famous for singing its beautiful songs at night. The nightingale also, according to Greek and Roman myth, alludes to the greek figure Philomel, who first had her own tongue cut from her mouth so that she would be unable to speak of the rape she had endured, and then is later turned into a nightingale by the grace of the gods so as to free her and help her escape death. Clearly this applies in numerous ways to both of the main characters. Isabelle on the one hand is actually named "the nightingale" in the story, and her last name, "Rossignol", is actually translated from the word "nightingale". Isabelle exhibits almost all of the things which the nightingale has come to represent; she is beautiful beyond measure, frequently yearns for the love of her family members as well as for Gaetan, works to free the world of its terrors and in the end, becomes, in a way, immortal herself through her memory which remains strong in the hearts of not just her family, but the family members of the hundreds of men she worked to save. Also, it is not a coincidence that the nightingale is famous for its song which it only sings at night, while Isabelle would move through the mountains with her

fallen air men doing her heroic brave work under the cover of night.

They symbol of the nightingale also can be seen as being relevant for Vianne too however, as Vianne exemplifies the myth of Philomel. Vianne, also having been raped, is stopped from ever discussing this with anyone via shame and regret. However, although she never reveals her secret, is, at the end of the novel, clearly no longer burdened deeply by what she has gone through. She has come to a place in her life where she can see the beauty in the events, as that was how she received her son who she claims brought her back to life.

The dead apple tree: Vianne's memory tree, the tree that she ties bits of cloth to to remember her dead or missing loved one, is the only tree in Vianne's garden which withers and dyes. This is clearly showing that Vianne's memories of her loved ones are fractured and shrouded in sorrow. While it is always a terrible thing to loose someone, Vianne chooses only to see the sadness in the losses and forgets to celebrate the lives that were lived and how they have affected her. She chooses to worry when she sees the tree instead of draw strength from it, and hence the memories in a way become a sort of disease ebbing its way into the life around it; hence the dead and wither tree which used to be full of life.

THEMES

Drastic seasonal changes: Throughout the story this is a very obviously recurring theme. The weather is harsh, being stifling hot in the summer and the winters bordering on unlivable, barren and cold. The point of these harsh seasons however is clear; despite what a person is going through, whatever hardships, life will continue to move on, as indifferent as ever to individual suffering. And while one could let the added stresses of living in extreme climate break them, to overcome and to have survived, allows one to further realize strength within themselves they may not have known they had.

Nationalism and War: These two are obvious as well, as nationalism is usually just something that goes hand in hand with war, war being the main theme throughout the books entirety. These two things set the stage for almost all of Isabelle's actions, and are also what drive Vianne to her eventual role in saving as many children as possible. These can also be seen within almost every character through the novel as affecting them all in major ways, whether it be by invoking feelings of supremacy in the Germans, invoking a desire to fight back in many citizens, or even simply in making it a matter of pride to refuse help from "the enemy".

Family: Again, this is a big one. The complex and somewhat untraditional family units that seem to exist within the lives of the characters plays a giant role in who each of the characters turn out to be, as well as in explaining, in a lot of cases, why the characters, specifically Vianne and Isabelle, are motivated to do the things they do and think the way they think, and in the end family is shown to be what is truly important and truly meaningful; the ultimate thing worth acting for.

REAL WORLD TRUTH

While the characters were fictional, as well as the town of Carrievau, what was not fictional was the type of suffering that occurred as well as the atrocities committed agains the French and Jewish civilians and people. Many of the bombings and experiences of women who had Germans Billeting at their homes, as well as the stories from the concentration camps, the examples of propaganda and the danger that surround every day life were all true. Also, Edith Cavell (Isabelle's idol), was in fact a very real person who is very much remembered and celebrated for her work during the first World War. Finally, many of the places that were mentioned were also very real. For example, the concentration camp Isabelle was sent to, Ravensbruck camp, was very real, as was the case also with the Pyrenees mountains, the Loire Valley, Paris and more.

THOUGHT PROVOKING MOMENTS

There are many moments throughout this book where one can see the tides turning or things that can be seen as character altering. These are just a few to consider.

-When Vianne writes the list of her colleagues for Beck and then is followed by immediate guilt and regret. Consider how this begins to change Vianne, who is used to following rules and authority without question. This is arguably the start of Vianne coming into her own as it helps her to realize that some things, just because an authority figure tells you to do them, are still wrong.

-Another moment along these same lines comes when Mother Superior Marie-Therese tells Vianne, after they have discussed her guilt for the list, that "as the war goes on we will have to look more deeply. These questions are not about them but about *us*... Don't think about who they are, think about who *you* are and what sacrifices you can make and what will break you". This is probably one of the most key passages to understanding the change the Vianne goes through, as well as helping the reader to also understand what many others are going through simultaneously; an identity crisis involving the deepest, most secret and desperate parts of their souls in regards to what they may have, or have already have, had to do to survive in their world.

-Consider also the first time that Isabelle tells Gaetan she loves him as apposed to the last. The first time you see a girl who is desperate to be loved in return, who is ruled by her passions and doesn't stop to consider what her actions might do. The last time she tells him however you see a woman who has come full circle, who fully understand what it is to love another, understand the consequences of all of her actions, and understanding who she truly is.

-Also consider the ending of the story, when everyone gathers to celebrate Isabelle. This is a very important moment because it clearly shows, possibly more than any other place within the novel, just how Isabelle has affected everyone around her. All she wanted was to be loved and remembered, and through her actions to save her country (which ironically she had to give up her family life to fulfill), not only is she both of these, but she has also saved more people, families and relationships than she could ever have imagined, helping to bring back to life many who fought in the war and would have been lost without her.

THOUGHTS FOR A PREQUEL
OR A SEQUEL

While it doesn't seem very plausible that a sequel could be written about Vianne, it is possible that one be written about the life that Gaetan, Ari or even Julien led after the war, as these were extremely interesting characters that it would have been enjoyable to get to know even further.

A prequel however could be most interesting! The novel talks a lot about how things used to be between Isabelle, Vianne, their father and mother before the war. It could be very interesting to see a novel written from the perspective of the now deceased mother of Isabelle and Vianne, as she too had to deal with the effects of war, a husband gone only to return in pieces, and two daughters, alone.

CONCLUSION/FINAL ANALYSIS

Overall this was an excellent novel. In a few places certain things could have been elaborated on or explained in more detail, (for example, Isabelle telling Gaetan she loves him for the first time came a bit out of the blue), however, over all expertly written. This is a very captivating novel that takes the reader of an exciting and original journey of the self-discovery, loss, bravery and eventual happiness of two seemingly opposite sisters who can and do find their way back to each other; a real page turner, to say the least.

CPSIA information can be obtained
at www.ICGtesting.com
Printed in the USA
LVOW04s1109270816

502113LV00019B/1134/P